The poems in *YEET!* act as incantations for hope, for life, for an "us." Through its variety of images, rhythms, and forms, *YEET!* saves room for joy, love, anger, sadness, healing, and yearning.
—Quintin Collins, author of *Claim Tickets for Stolen People* and *The Dandelion Speaks of Survival*

YEET! is a vibrant and powerful collection that prods at the future sacred and meditates on the archive of our own choosing. In poems that transfigure or vanish before our eyes, crawford invites the reader into the contagious energy of their world—a place where the scaffolding is Black, collective, and alive.
—Rio Cortez, author of *Golden Ax*

There is an intense cosmic energy required to do what jason b crawford's *YEET!* does: to give life and love to that impossible, yet constant, toggle between that which cannot be said, and that which cannot be ignored. It tenderly holds the complexity of being Black and queer in the kind of country where Skittles can be heartbreaking. It tends marigolds and dahlias, right in the breach. Violence, beauty, smoke. Poetic craft runs deep and deft, exploratory. We ponder what to do with the "dirt-spit bouquet." The reader is carried—from intimate poems of friendship and love, to the vast horizon—"small petals of lavender cleaning the sky of its grief." When not carrying the beat of a party, with all its overtones and undertones, the poems pulse with quiet grace and heat. This book is a radiant, intergalactic, hot bloom of a fire—it is so much love.
—Sawako Nakayasu, author of *Pink Waves*, judge's citation for Omnidawn 2022 1st/2nd Book Contest

YEET! is a collection of departures and arrivals where all roads lead to love. Guided by a heart that uses form, homage, and boundless lyric to lead the way, be prepared to exit these poems with wings added to your spirit. No, you're not dead. You're headed someplace magnificent, baby. jason b crawford is a bright star in the darkest corner of night. Follow them. These poems are lanterns, check-points, medicine, and shelter in the rough and cruel terrain of our shared today.
—Danez Smith, author of *Bluff*

This butt-kick of a book, penned by one of contemporary poetry's most insisting demagogues, is grounded by one poem's memorable opening line: i start every story with noticing. In *YEET!*, that act of witnessing is in turn single-minded, mournful, merciless, hurtful or threaded with black boy joy. As we stumble through a new world where truth is in such short supply, let's be thankful that jason steadfastly refuses the safety of silence as they confront the crusade to disappear Black history, the villainy of wars, and the battles we fight ceaselessly within ourselves. These are poems that must be confronted and lived—enter their lyric with your mind wide open, and let a consummate witness tell you what they've learned.
—Patricia Smith, author of *The Intentions of Thunder: New and Selected Poems*

YEET!

Poems

Cover art by jason b crawford

Interior design by jason b crawford and Laura Joakimson
Interior typefaces:Times New Roman and Cardo

Library of Congress Cataloging-in-Publication Data
Names: Crawford, Jason B. (Poet) author
Title: Yeet! : poems / Jason B. Crawford.
Description: Oakland, California : Omnidawn Publishing, 2025. | Summary: "Following the traditions of Eve L. Ewing, Rio Cortez, and Douglas Kearney, Jason B. Crawford's YEET! envisions the Black community lifted off the earth and set free towards the stars. These poems ask what a free Black people would look like and how we might achieve such a thing. This collection presents a new take on Afrofuturism and utopianism. Rather than looking to a future of technological change, it steps years ahead to show how people are happier once they are no longer owned. These poems speak to racism, gun violence, colonization, global warming, flight, joy, friendship, and noise. This is a book about creating new worlds without the systems of supremacy that held down the old one. YEET! is the winner of the 2023 Omnidawn 1st/2nd Poetry Book Contest, chosen by Sawako Nakasayu"-- Provided by publisher.

Identifiers: LCCN 2025024902 | ISBN 9781632431707 trade paperback | ISBN 9781632431936 ebook
Subjects: LCGFT: Poetry
Classification: LCC PS3603.R39632 Y44 2025 | DDC 811/.6--dc23/eng/20250625
LC record available at https://lccn.loc.gov/20250249

Published by Omnidawn Publishing, Oakland, California
www.omnidawn.com
10 9 8 7 6 5 4 3 2 1
ISBN: 978-1-63243-170-7

YEET!

Poems

jason b crawford

Omnidawn Publishing
Oakland, California
2025

This bitch empty… YEEEEEEEEET!

—Vine Girl 2014

they smashed a bottle on the squad cars—a Hennessy bottle or
Coke or a pressed kale juice, whatever was near enough to say 'this
here is   christened a new thing'

—Eve L. Ewing ~ *Arrival Day*

Nigger, read this and run!
Now, if you can't read,
run anyhow!

—James Baldwin ~ *Staggerlee Wonders*

no need for geography
now, we safe everywhere

—Danez Smith ~ *summer, somewhere*

Contents

When we finally get there——
after George Abraham

1.
—should we start by crafting a map? I must be honest, I do not know where in the galaxy *there* is. I do not know the lineage for this soil, no clear placement of meteors to name where we have been or where we have yet made it safe. Traversing the long Atlantic of the stars is tiring when done correctly. I know there are planets unnamed by bad hands, ones too far to spit at our Nike-crescent smiles. I know my beloveds are willing to travel space in search for them. Not sure the shape of the rock we will call home, but I know it will be magnificent and rich, brimming with dirt. Finally we can count all that is ours.

2.
—what part of our inventory will be colonized? What parts of this land can we say we own? What we found, what we remember most during travel, must have been the rotting cherries devoted to the most beautiful trees. The hydrangea-light licking at the stems, hugging each root. The raspberries climbing the trunks of our legs in preparation for their own exploration. What we found here was beauty in the form of *everything been free*. Nothing was ever theirs.

3.
—we will not call any of our findings *ours*, just brother, sister, mother, friend, bush of knowing I refuse to steal from; a stone swallowing a stone, swallowing a stone; endless; forever-planet sized gobstopper floating in between nowhere and *we are too far gone*; here everything could be different if we stopped believing in gravity, if the ashes of all borders were tucked beneath the carpet, if we forgot the language of taking, if they hadn't the ability to travel here first—

Departure

I can't stop singing
                folk songs about you
and by you
        I mean
                anywhere but here
                        —Rio Cortez "The Creature Describes Her Own Hands"

essay on YEET!

an archival after Douglas Kearney

i • saw • the •
bullet • take
•aim•take•flight•take•towards•
the • flesh • crave • the • body •
sweet • scalpel • the • insides • of
muscle • weave • the • deltoid • •
through • the • pectoralis • pattern
perform • dance • twirl • among •
•bones•polish•around•the blood
•its • brass • shell • swept • •clean
• throughout • the •
body collect • the
•dust•as•it•folded••the•arteries
• into • a • buckling laughter • i •
marveled • at • its
• • meticulousness
• matronly • nature to • lick • the •
wound • it • just • • split •
open

in the new world there will not be a gun or a fist shaped into a gun or a mouth

screaming like a gun or a toy perceived to be a gun or a pack of candy

loaded like a gun or a bag pretending to be a gun or a jury

that convicts like a gun or

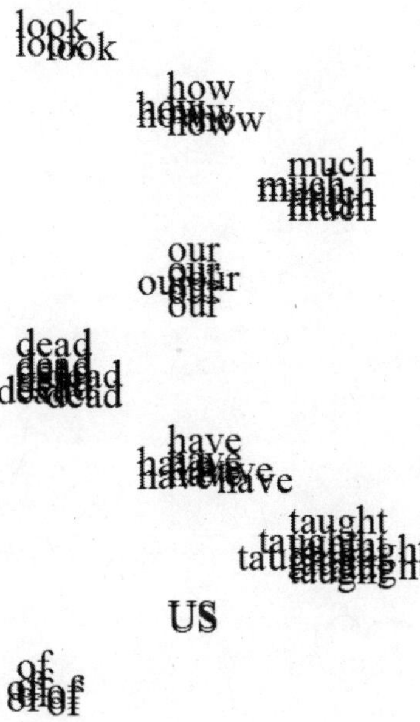

survival.

Exhaustion Theory

This city lacks the space for me
to yell or sing at my loudest   when I am lonely. How likely
                    one could confuse my sadness
for exhaustion if I let them; I never say   a word.   There is an echo
I wish to own; the midnight air   in Ypsilanti parking lots could tender this
sweet to my tongue. Too often I think   about grief.   Once I wasn't afraid.   In a poem
I wrote "I understand leaving," and a chorus   of doorways appeared
everywhere around me. I fell   through, sought the aftermath   of baby's breath. Refused
to calculate the risk of being   a____ too close to what   we called purity. Purified
myself in that bed made   from silted petals,   guilted laughter. There is so much
that could have k_____ me without   my knowledge, and I do not give   them praise. Most gods
have brought me to these uncertainties,   yet I bow still, to show   faith/to save   face. The lies
here are unending/unreliable. I do   fear, I always have. I always will. I fear leaving more
now than ever. But I've practiced vulnerability, placed the act
in my mouth, a small film   projected from my teeth that I title
<u>times I should have cried but didn't</u>. *Sometimes I pretend to cry at the safest part of the movie.*   The script would say.

Sometimes the credits roll and the lights dawn and I'm still in the front row, unable to leave,

violently weeping.

notice theory

i start every story with noticing: what i can touch, who i cannot. i take survey of the room, question who is alive, who might be a figment of my false reality.

often i do not believe someone is dead until i call them and they do not answer. when i was a child, i thought everyone was dead until they appeared in front of me, risen from the grave.

what vast variance i've created for myself through this learning of deadness. i tell a friend to *text me when you make it home* and they do not. in my mind they are gone. i find a dead hen in the pond knee-deep in ice. i am not sure about the protocol of dead things. i do not touch it.

i believe in omens. i believe in the pith of mothers saying text me when you get home, chile, i believe in the dragging of the "l" in "chile" to emphasize how tired we have become at losing kin to the night air—i answer every message within seconds, to prove my existence. i speak invocations of survival, place runes beneath my tongue in prayer. *let my grandfather be okay when he misses my phone call. let my sister be okay when she forgets to message me back.*

even for my father, whom i do not call, i still pray. i search his name in the toledo papers, wait to hear from his wife that he did not make it; that she sat, phone in hand, waiting for the text that would not arrive.

on the other hand, my mother texts me every morning just to prove to herself she is not a ghost. i answer every message seconds after i receive it. on the days she does not respond to my response, i spend the rest of the day waiting for her eulogy.

essay on YEET!

an archival after Xan Phillips

dear world i am learning   quietness   here
the word   is a storm that tantrums until it is a soft tempered
rain   what good is this violence when   only leads
to more violence   i am afraid   i bleed
like a fragile balloon   i am not   without
fault   i have taken from others   i have missed a call
home to my grandmother   more than once   i have sped
sometimes without destination   i have traced the cracks
in a water pitcher and started to mourn   and stopped
believing   in hope in silence i, golden child, try my hand at
considering the law   how to be a "good
black" to not run   towards nor away
nor at all considering the silence   again in this   lack
of movement how to not be   to stay   still stay
unnoticed   there is death   in this silence there is
death   to be considered in everyone mine could be blue
bullets   burrowing through my chest
learning   the body most fit for its meal   a gut swollen from
silence   then the body breaks   a palm fissuring
a thrashing creak   the shell of me shatters
to grit   i fear the river's blue hands
guiding me towards   the bullet   i am a burgeoning
engine slicing my fingers   to softness   i wrought the skin
to bone   can the law save me   from anyone but myself
misguided   fool readied to call the soil
so come reaper   come   bring   me   home

This Has Never Been My america

I could talk about every video clip of bodies rolling on pavement, skin-smeared sidewalks, the hopscotch of our bones. But what would it do, other than incite a riot in my stomach? I do believe in abolition, yet have never been a fan of sticking my own hands in the mud. Does this make me a bad Black, the type soft white lips have not warned their children about? All of my (white) partners' parents loved me, some even far after our parting. They used to say *it's so sad what happened to that boy, but do you all have to keep looting?* and all I could offer was a concerned grin, minstrel-toothed and tame. I don't know what I am waiting for. A free, borderless land? A space for all my niggas to be niggas? I'm sure on top of a mountain somewhere there are collections of us made god, allowed to crack in peace, crack into the hands of their own loved ones and gust into a darkening red sky. The living, the dead, their names all never etched on a baton of tongues. I am optimistic about what it could look like if we didn't know anything but the dark. I am waiting to forget why we reach for the light.

could
I stick my hands in
the bad white ? All my (white) partners'
loved parting The *boy*
and all I could offer was a minstrel . I don’t know free,
space my niggas be niggas collections
to crack in the hands
on a baton . I know the dark I am waiting
to forget .

I
have
warned
you all
.
all my niggas be
dead names
on tongues. we know
why .

If I ever leave New York, I am going to burn everything

I own. This is where the stork left
me, at the foot of a planet learning to murder

itself. Before, I traced along Michigan's long blue
veins, found a clean passageway

home. I was built in a forest of boys slap—
boxing the summer's sweat. Now, a colosseum

of staggering buildings stretch
inwards towards me, their fingers

mushroomed and unwanting. Their awkward
gaze sticking to me like too-ripe fruit. They must

teach me about my skin and its dysfunction, the walls
I refuse to blend into, what happens when I can be seen,

I am a child—

born in a country that hates me more
than I hate myself. I'm trying to understand the color

green, all the life that it could hold, but I cannot shake this feeling of what I owe.

essay on YEET!

after Hanif Abdurraqib

i pass a creek
that is still spitting up salmon
to offer to its lover, the pond
that sends back its own salivic gifting:
a constant exchange
of gratitudes. my fingers kiss a slab
of bark and ask only that my children can live
half as long. that must be the point
of all this war, to understand
the durability of trees. i lie still
enough to let a cardinal nest upon the divot
in my shoulder and lay her eggs
and ain't that what it means to trust god?
to bring life into a world
that looks to take you out with
a single stone?

If I keep saying flowers in enough poems, I wonder if they'll finally bloom

My manager speaks to me about manifestations, about how to make money
grow beneath the wilted fingers of dead men. She talks
prayer and candles and bay leaves while I'm still here daydreaming
about the marigolds I tuck behind my bottom lip. The dirt

grows beneath the wilted fingers of dead men. She talks
of my mouth, the gums that don't seed flowers well no matter how hard I try to
marigold the leaves I tuck behind my bottom lip. The dirt-
spit bouquet. Maybe it is time to acknowledge that

my mouth doesn't gum the seed of these flowers well, no matter how hard I try.
She is right about the water in the wording. I start to speak
spit bouquets, start to acknowledge the
dahlias appearing everywhere, like an incantation—

she is right about the water in the wording. I start to speak
encyclopedias of faith, write in the grease on my arms.
Dahlias appearing everywhere, without explanation.
I say daffodil and become a florist carving out my loves' shapes in an

encyclopedia of blossoming faith. Write in the grease
of my yellow silt, say iris and let its petals crawl down my throat.

expand into a silvered leaflet on my tongue. I say this all
to bed bois in my soiled lungs; sludge the equator of my esophagus;
Black boi, Queer boi, Flower boi;

expand a silvered leaflet on my tongue. I say
their names
and when I swallow a handful of sunflower seeds
my dead manifest from my mouth;

If I ever leave New York, I am going to burn everything

mapping my death. Watch america play
cartographer; again, drawing lines across what

I do not own. Watch america play
butcher, slicing red down

my sides, delicate meat
of ancestry. The tapestry of stories

this country wishes
not to remember. Let's call it

redlining, redistricting, removing the stains
of brown left out in the sun. When I leave I want

to ignite the blood-drawn lines and watch
them disappear behind the flame.

I want them to know
I was here.

Quick:

someone

teach me

the word

for sick

or blood

or terminal.

How else will I know

what I have lost

A Triple Sonnet for the Lost

for Dorothy Chan

everything the light touches becomes
        light; spiraling backwards. skulls of grey
wolves, elephant husks, beaver tails
        all planted in gloves of our mother's willing
knees. we prayed to get somewhere
        and somewhere we got. found
a new name for joy and all of her
        beautiful singing sisters, o shaped mouths
praising the glory of becoming ghost. o' glory
        we have been here before; been made
a hymn out of a boi/a dress/a frozen tongue
        been in search of what we forever called
the promised land. turned stone to boat to
        ship tossed across the heavy oceaned sky

a ship was tossed across the heavy ocean sky
        into what most would claim to be oblivion's
sweet kiss. but we know death like a lover.
        how to hold them close,   wield them
like a blunted blade. why must this all
        seem so familiar; this catching of specters
flying loose from my father's wrinkling
        hands. we sought space and chose space
  and found space   where,
        we will never tell. but i can say, here it is
beautiful, these masterful pine trees; old oaks
        full of green stories and too-long laughs;
we made it; but now we haven't much time; just
        look at where the outline of the waterfalls

look at where the outline of the water
        chases the toes of the land;
can you not see it? over in the distance,
        my grandmother's scooping cackle
my grandfather's drying legs buckled over
        Tiran, dressed in two hundred gold links
the edges of our love's brilliant
        bodies pressed against the ocean bed
listen to them sing, all of them
        even the ones i refuse to name, again
listen to them, so loud, so bright
        so brown and glitter-covered, sing
"we are free" "we are free" "we are home"
        everything the light could touch we become

essay on YEET!

the invisible city after Italo Calvino

this city: a houseparty with all my friends, all Black, swaying
to “No Hands,” all understanding the lyrics,
nigga want beef? we can take it outside
and around me is only niggas, so we say
nigga
but mean *my love*, we say
my niggas
and that ownership ain’t about owning shit, we say
my niggas
and we mean *my niggas*
are a national anthem, a country of Black
a porous harmony, *girl the way you movin’, got me in a trance,*

and i argue

that Wale got the best sixteen of summer 2010 and the door to our island
of Black swings

open and brings in more Black and notice the music-video stank
drifting out the basement apartment on Pearl St, the hush
of violins whispering for us

to get close during "Everything
to Me" and i'll mention the sweat

of Henny Dougie'n through the jungle juice; it is the one summer
we all bumped to Fatty Koo's "Bounce," replayed "Ready to Die,"
pretended

like we were, in fact, ready
to die and we know this party will only last

until about 1:15 am before the cops roll up and we roll

out in packs, in bunches, the thin cry of our cackles sweetening

the mid-September air, and we are all of age but still fear
the haunt of blue wandering the Ypsilanti streets and this

is pre Eric Garner but post Oscar Grant
and we have been Black

before which just means we understand the metrics
of a bullet. no one in this poem is allowed to die
in the arms of anyone else at this party and it hasn't hit

midnight yet so our laughter has not become an inconvenience, which means
we are still
invisible and how else am i to interpret joy if not through all this

laughter? through all these niggas so close
that we create a Black hole—
a hurricane—
                    a night storm—

and i cannot write the names of my loves
that were in attendance because if i put them
on paper this becomes a elegy, but know
we were all there running
into the pitch dark summer, the night
catastrophied

by
our
laughter.

and in this poem, more flowers

a recipe

Run your feet across a field of April lilacs; like a German shepherd, curious, stuff
your nose into the flower's blunt pad and sneeze away its petals, their collage
purpling the wind. What wonder. Create more angels in this field's chalky
pollen, arms flailing in the grass until the golden-hued dirt picks up
on your jean jacket. Marvel at the grave you just dug, the imprint
of a moving thing photographed mid-flight. Place a few
of the lilacs in a paper bag. Something must die

in this poem; let it be by your learned hands. Spread a few
scant stems around your garden, bless your home with their
drying limbs. Scoop a jarful of river from your backyard, place each
remaining stem in the jar and kiss it with sunlight. Watch the leaves twitch,
drink in desperation. If there isn't enough water for them to survive, you have to
fill a small plot under the oak with ashes; praise what can be learned from this near-
dying. Know you will still wake the next morning.

essay on YEET!

a conjuring after Dior J Stephens

in the world there are bullets
in the new world there are no bullets
in the new world there are no bullets
in the new world there are no bullets
in the new world there are no bullets
in the new world there are no bullets
in the new world there are no bullets
in the new world there are no bullets
in the new world there are no bullets
in the new world there are no bullets
in the new world there are no bullets
in the new world there are no bullets
in the new world there are no bullets
in the new world there are no bullets
in the new world there are no bullets
in the new world there are no bullets
in the new world there are no bullets
in the new world there are no bullets
in the new world there are

Arrival

We built that.
Isn't that our story? To be denied
the beginning.
—Rio Cortez "I Learn to Shoot a Bow"

if i cannot find our safety anywhere in this galaxy, then i will become Nowhere

i am unable to evaluate this rain's consistency; it drowns my throat
in thought, a flush of pebbles watershed from my mouth. if the light begat
the earth then so shall my open jaw, my gold teeth that bright this land with a single
smile. i become a new country, skin blistered into mountain ranges; the first flesh to break
deteriorated into soil, a good brown. the hairs on my arms and chest sprouted into trees, my pubic
hair a jungle of fresh bark. the hairs on my shins marsh with cattails and glasswort. my nails make marble,
limestone, obsidian, things to carve into an ax. antelope gallop the length of my sternum bucking into each
other's brash skulls. through the cornea, bloodlight moons over the raccoons, possums fish beneath the threads
in my iris, hummingbirds fold between the water plantains on my thighs, their bristled wings cutting through
the warm summer song. and what of the bugs? ants dig into the pockets of my shoulders, dragonflies nestle
on milkweed roots made from my eyelashes. they too live in the small hairs around my lips and chin,
a woodland stuffed with deer springing new antlers. my meadowed cheeks now a bloody velvet.
if i do not make it, can i become a place where the rest of my people survive?

Gettin' Religion, 1948

after Archibald John Motley Jr

sip—singe our lips an unbloodied red—swing—sing—smooth—groove—
sax-filled—the night tries to swallow everything but the sound we got and we
raucous, we loud as houndstooth and we jive—like them old men and them young
men and them old men that was once young and we all young and we Black
the block with our noise and they listen from they windowsills, winter long
done left they mouths and they grab they dancing shoes and they dancing
partners too and we color and colored and blue-Black and blew black from
our lungs and we curved-hipped and spit-slick at the ankles; we impossible
dark, we mama fried it good, greaseshine babies, clay inheritance; we bestiaries
of beautiful findings, thickets of long tooths, the sloppiest unchecked grins, we perfect
round, crimson cut our lips and we resist   saying *alive* here or anywhere
we survive; call it taboo to be alive or aware of being anywhere—we want
to bask in that dusk-sound them children make—what night done gave us. music.
what i mean here is that we want that music to catch us by our tongues.

History of the Ark

A pop quiz

1. And as all things do, this must start…

{a} in fire—kissing the calves of our brick homes. So easily
spread was the french-tongued flame. Embers cascading
the clay-smeared doors.

{b} in Pompeiiing the bent frame of the earth's crust. A world
ravaged by its own copper lungs. Stones loud enough to crack
a glass wake wide open.

{c} in a gust of wind aimed at our bodies. Parallel
to the tearing of the earth's paper bones. All that
is laid in ash and dust and gold debris spreading across the sea.

{d} in leaving.

2. *I've gathered enough lineage…*

{a} to string together the origin of my birth. Its wet diligence, heavy in my palms. How to decipher the blood without spilling it, before the mess of what hands can offer in return.

{b} to know I do not belong among so few maple trees. I am a full growing willow, split at the curl of my smile.

{c} to watch the beads of my mother's mother's mother scatter across the wood floor. And in this I understand leaving—fabricating enough limbs to build a bridge or boat or ladder or javelin or anything solid enough to carry my people home.

{d} to question the legitimacy of a name.

3. *At first it was simple…*

{a} to gather my kin by their tendering roots. My potted fingers, tiny shovels showing what love is capable of when given back the tools (even after the rot has set).

{b} to till the oak, fold the dirt, mine the air, make the craft, salt the wood, build the glue, brace the throat, fill the mouth, sharpen the water, lift the sound, till the, fold the, mine the, make the, salt the, build the, brace the, fill the, sharpen the, fold, salt, build, fill, lift, make, fill, and lift and lift and lift and lift and

{c) to question the possibilities of rain. We deluged the eyes until we were our own desert bowl, scooped from the moistening sand. We pulled meat from the sunflower stems and this we called the feast, made sloppy by our mangled arms.

{d} to pull the ocean towards us by its feet.

4. The first question asked was…

{a} do we start by crafting a map?

{b} how do we carry our dead in our mouths?

{c} do we know when in space we will land?

{d} how do we choose whom to leave behind?

Ode to Bear Milk

and if we can pause for
a second to talk about Black
bodies close enough to pass heat
between their furred chests; a furnace of boys
warming each other through an already too hot
summer evening; light fractaling across a stone floor
as a whole club uncloseets itself into clanking
chimes; a golden film silhouetting the fluorescent bodies
in sweat; someone's son,
                    or daughter,
                                        or unnamed
body snakes across the dance floor to touch the swelling of another's
jaspilite arms; in this tiny heatbox club there is more body than space given;

there is always more

boy to split open with our rigid tongues
                                                  like fresh pomegranates;
flesh expanding into each other; and who am i to not call this beautiful? these old
pipes unwinding into each other; a crashing symphony of musk dragging its way between us;
i watch a soft silver boi as he trinkets around the men;
                                             another damselflies his tongue into another's mouth

and another steals the stench off another's glistening armpits
                                                            and another glows a bright heat in line for
his undoing at the sex tent and
                                        another crawls his way backwards up a wall, knees stilted against
the brick as he swamps the floor beneath him in his dance
and another   and another   and another   and another   and another   and another   and another   a n d
another   and another
and another   and another   and another   and another   and another   and another   and another   a n d
another
and another   and another   and another   and another   and another   and another   and another   a n d
another   and another
and another   and another   and another   and another   and another   and another   and another   a n d
another
and another   and another   and another   and another   and another   and another   and another   a n d
another   and another
and another   and another   and another   and another   and another   and another   and another   a n d
another
and another   and another   and another   and another   and another   and another   and another   a n d
another   and another
and   and   and   and   and   and   and   and
and
and   and   and   and   and   and   and   and
and
and   and   and   and   and   and   and   and
and

and and and and and and and and
and and and and and and and and
and
and and and and and and and and
and
and and and and and and and and
and
and and and and and and and and
and and and and and and and and
and
and and and and and and and and
and
and and and and and and and and
and
and and and and and and and and
and and and and and and and and
and
and and and and and and and and
and
and and and and and and and and
and
and and and and and and and a n d

and and and and and and and and
and

and and and and and and and and
and
and and and and and and and
and and
and and and and and and and
and
and and and and and and and and
and
and and and and and and and and
and

essay on YEET!

on tenderness
after Camonghne Felix

Today, I am relearning
        tenderness—its porosity. The weight
of the past folds safely in my
        palms, its playful blades rest
upon the nape of my neck; I know
        this is love, this cutting. Deep
down, I know it wants
        what is best for me. I give it
blood. I used to write grief into
        every poem, but not
today. Instead, I'll finally think
        of the chrysanthemums, fill the vase
of my chest until I can only exhale
        bees and honey. Praise
this warmth I don't know
        will return tomorrow.
Small blessings I forget
        to relearn; more

times than not, I fall
        victim to my own body's wants;
I am a requiem
        of trout; a boi's mouth hooked on what
smells like rain. Do not try
        to teach me the ocean's greed, I am well versed
in its chaining. Don't preach
        to me in the savior's bellowing
tongue, I've long been one tangled
        with the trees. Don't tell me about the boats.
I was made from this soil
        and I replant myself
every day; I am sprouting
        a new set of bones; maybe this time
I'll add wings.
        I am relearning
definitions of love. Replaced
        every picture in my house with my own
skin. Notice its rigid
        bark; it's so tender
the touch; tender the meat
        of the wood, tender the flame;

Asters

somehow the language of these maps has changed. I can no longer read

the directions of our linear time. Often, I wonder if we should

make a discography of distance. Catalog different ways of leaving

without leaving one's self behind; I dawn

from a world built on crosses aching

for a flame's stubborn mouth; I think of all the ways

they chose to break us in;

there, held sickness

and sickness and sickness and sickness and

sickness and no one could tell

any of them apart well enough to perform

the healing; we sought

grief like a harpooned whale, a clean incision

into land's skull; what beauty

we found, dying in pursuit of eternity. Somehow,

the rain is more vibrant

here, the trees have learned to blossom inward; a spiral

of vibrantly mauve asters whisper to us

nightly, *take care/take care/take care*; I cannot help

but to think my grandmother sits on the star of their petals wishing

me a safe and long journey home; I lay

hyacinths at the foot of each year

for her as we call a new place home. What will this look like

next fall, when we all live past

the summer's blade?

If I ever leave New York, I am going to burn everything;

and if it were to be that simple, I'd spark
a match between the twigs
of my two fingers, watch the purple flame spread
up my elbow and caress the shoulder's fat, let it bite

softly at the crown of my neck, the smoke choking
me out like only a good love would. By everything,
I mean to include myself on this pyre
of small disasters. The thin grease of want

stoking the white heat. I am learning how to burn
a house down from the inside. Let's take it from there,
from the top. The reincarnation of my blood
pooling in another man's mouth. What we mistake

for lust is often a form of colonization
in action. I have seen what fire can devastate
in capable hands. I've stopped questioning
where I belong, how long

before something with more water comes
to fizzle me out. This world aches to
find ways to undo my skin. Has been taught
how to smolder Black skin. I, too, have asked

for labor from myself that now seems unjust
in its intent. I can never be that white boy
I’ve told myself to love. How sad
I must have been to keep this pyre in me

burning until I was nothing
but ash. Maybe this is the only
true way to leave, find a new land.
I want to know what is different there:

bois of inflammable carbon limbs;
bois of the rising heat’s dark, cold kiss;
bois pulled from the gut of the flame,
still scorched by smoking lips.

Essay on YEET!

a scorched cento

—should we start by crafting a map? i can no longer read
the directions of our linear time. i am a burgeoning engine sometimes
without destination. watch me play cartographer; again i am drawing
lines across what i do not own. who am i to question what is safe
here? i used to write grief into every poem. it drowns
my throat in thought, a flush of pebbles
watershed from my mouth; i once loved
america, too. i once thought love an infinite. split.
open. I am learning how to burn a house down from the inside. i speak
of the trees and mean the dead air rapturing my hands. I watch
its petals bullet out towards my skin. i do not have more
to spare. i mean none of us ever exist at all.

A Double Sonnet for the River

and because this is a poem about joy, it too must have a river flowing
from its greedy jaws. i have only learned how to speak about joy
as an offering to a god i will never understand. i once watched a fire
hydrant open its locked-turned throat and flood the city in what
i mistook to be the fresh smell of the thornapple; and because
of my own instinct, i expected a school of children, wide in their grins
and teeth fencing about their gums, to swim towards the cracked
basin, searching for salvation, cooling their mouths with the sharp taste
of nickel, and because I am reminded of my childhood, chasing a spitting
sprinkler head in my front yard or of the trips to the houghton lake
that held shores of loose sand that could swallow a child whole but we chose
to stomach the dirt gripped at our feet, treading the deepest palm of the
shallow end while our parents watched from the beach just as how I now
watch these children choosing to defy the act of drowning; typical how
they sought what once killed us, how it is now ailing their dry tongues.

and because this is a poem
about joy, i trust the river
to hold me longer
than could the ocean's
open barrelled hands.
i trust no god like i do
my own people,
if i am to die, let it be
in the presence
of the ones that
loved me most, let me drown
in their mouths and
continue flowing
through their veins

History of Leaving

a pop quiz

1. How did the great migration begin?

we cannot talk about history without mentioning its war-
drawn blades. the famine sought by the rifle's empty tongue
prodding at our skin. i wish to say migration was new
to us, that we learned to leave by leaving; but it started
with the first fire, years before i could remember the taste
of breath. to sum it up: there was a war, people died,
we left by boats and force. our bodies refracted by the sparks
of the barrel's fluorescent smoke. everyone's history has blood
running from its hands. we pooled ours
until we could fuel our way home.

2. What was lost in the first fire?

the flames were their own
displacement, their own hunger-filled mules, spreading
across our homes. some of us survived. again,
we are talking about a history of chance. my ancestors hushed
under floorboards before the fifth war, traced the moon's river
to safety. prayed for the luck of a missed bullet, for the quiet
child stowed in the thick night. my mother built me
from survival.

3. How can you describe the journey to the new land?

why question the spectacle? once there was
a flock of birds, brilliantly painting a grey sky. we reached towards them
and they scooped us into their bronze beaks, carried us somewhere
safer. let someone much lighter tell it, they would
call this escaping. every mouth retells it
differently. what story can you crack open
and not find a grinning fox,
blood running from its gums?

the first national anthem: the last elegy

we no longer carry cardamom to house parties, instead we gift
the front lawn with cloves tumbleweeding from our hands. present

the open veins of leaves as a peace treaty. we question
every invitation with invitation; no home is left unwelcome,

a clutch of vanilla orchids dug into our creaking elbows. often we wonder
when dying became an option. we haven't taken the time to understand

the weight of flour. when we were younger, our grandmothers would weigh
with their hands and it would always be enough; never a moment in rolling

out the dough would they interrogate the measurements, add more
milk to the bowl, watch the paste drown into a chalky soup.

it's easy to question the legitimacy
of an anthem, but aren't all anthems just elegies

and aren't all elegies just recipes
left by our mother's splintered wooden spoons?

we praise no god in this new land, but every mother's kitchen
hum becomes the holiest worship. what else to bestow upon a troubled

people other than rum and garlic, wings and brandy, joy
and breathing—freedom singing from the skillet's popping tongue.

“Life before the war was beautiful”

after Kuzbass Zubrii

orchids could fold from the plots in our hands, spin themselves into a gorgeous golden ribbon, wrap the necks of all the neighborhood’s children. a glistening fireshow ruptured between the old apartment complexes, the corner stores, the liquor stores, the ice cream shops; if it had the potential, it lit to smoke, would carry our dust to the next town over. every evening a parade of boys with starfish constellating their scalps cackled into the mouth of a summer breeze. the scent of their roll call oceaned the entire city in a chorus calling back, *hootie hoo*. what a way to say we are safe, by the sky buoyed in our honest smiles, the clouds wringing with want; the walls lush with burgundy polyester. trees flooded our oldsmobile backdrops with rose stems, a group of obsidian girls painted the skyline in salt. with the haunt of a north star hiding behind the sun, we became impossible.

"On God"

essay on Language

> Thou shalt not take the name
> of the Lord thy God in vain;
> for the Lord will not hold him
> guiltless that taketh his name in vain.
> —Exodus 20:7

We have all done it / in the sweat-licked heat of summer / thought of the ways an ice-cold Gatorade / could coat the tail end of the throat / and made a promise to our savior / in exchange for moistened lips / How we quote scripture in our language / about the bodies made of matches / We speak of the soft-memoried fables / around crashing beer bottles / and hollerin' mouths gaping with spit / circlin' a campfire mid-July / We say *On God*, and it means / *I promise everything to you / or equally nothing at all* / We sit in the presence of the dinner table / bellies full of collards and cornbread / and we say *On God / this is the best meal that has ever been made* / our grandmas / hands readied / in a spatula-whip position / snips to not use the Lord / name in vain / but we only mean it as a hymn / *On God I promise / On God, I will fight / to keep all those around me alive / all of this family / and friends that are family / that I break my body into bread for / On God, I mean oh God / I mean this is not in vain / I pray / I pray / I pray / I am enough / to feed them*

translations of an ancient text

for Chris L. Butler

in the new world we still say *jawn*

as in {n.} the spot,
{n.} the lick,
{n.} the good good,
{n.} the what i need
at this moment.

as in {v.} the words i forget
are special until i am holding them
again in my arms.

we still say *we done*...

as in {adj.} inevitable.

as in {v.} never question
our mother's capable hands.

as in {v.} she breaks the chicken
at the joint, severs the spine, always finds
enough for two meals in one split bone.

in the new world we retired:

the word {n.} *cop*, and {n.} {v.} *police*, and {n.} *prison*, and {v.} *remain silent,* and {v.} *silencing*, and a list of words we no longer need to govern us, like {n.} government, or {n.} president, or {n.} whiteness.

we still say *what's gud, g?*

as in {n.} hello my love
that i cannot name
in public.

as in {v.} i am here
for you to talk or not talk about it all.

as in {v.} let me unfold
the table of my palms and bring sweet fruit to your mouth.

as in {adj.} i'm choosing to ungroom this tongue
for you. blessed boy running from his own chalk shadow.

as in {adj.} i'm sorry
i do not have more
to spare.

essay on YEET!

a friendship poem after Sam Herschel Wein

When I am sad I grow my hair to its tallest
branch; some nights, I call over

Sam J. and Patrick and Taylor and Gardy and Stephen
and Payton and Aubrey and Dee and Sam H. and we gossip

about boys; stupid boys with their stupid
names and why they are so often

the lineage for this foliage. Sam J. braids my hair
back into a thick of vines for Patrick to swaddle

around his naked neck. Stephen chooses the movie
that is just right, Gardy pulls the boxed pizza

from the oven. Payton dresses our cocktails with blueberries,
bouquets flowering from the glasses. Dee paints freckles

on the back of my arm in the shapes of constellations he remembers
from when he was a child; we all gleam under the ublongness

of the moon and Aubrey requests that it returns
the next night no matter how sad or

less sad we may become. Taylor reminds me that
I do not own sadness; it does not belong to my body,

but sometimes we borrow it; Sam H. jokes
and it, too, is just right—the amount of laughter, how it holds

in the mouth, all of us open-jawed and laughing
until the room swells and the door swings open—

and it is Joshua. He, too, now is laughing, is now part
of this lineage of hurt, the walls shaking from our convulsions.

I could end the poem there, at the buckling
of bodies hot as a Florida night, or I could add more

bodies to this too-small apartment: Dior
and Jim and Joy and Zora and Fey and

Daniel and Kay and Jovan and Michelle and
Alexis and Amber and Chas and Matthew and

mention the A/C that was not built to carry

this much heat and mention the fear

soaking the room. We worry
that someone here today might not be here

tomorrow and isn’t it funny how a poet mentions blood
and everyone leans in, salivating? There are some days

I am so lonely that all I can do is sit on the edge
of my bed and cry until flowers sprout

underneath my pillow. Some days there is no poetry
in the way I speak; those are my saddest days.

Some days I forget my friends, or that I have friends
to forget, until I chip away at the paint

on my walls and hear the sound of my friends
chuckling uncontrollably back at the moon.

Ars Poetica

i know,   i know   what a gorgeous world i've built
in this aftershock; i mention the trees and they rot, how beautiful
is that? i've carried some of my people on my tongue and left the rest
dry. gambled with who   was supposed
to survive. i've folded the poem into a boat safe enough
for my loves to drown   by my side. i've tested
the buoyancy of paper, money or otherwise; all turn
transparent as lungs. i must   apologize
for acting on what could have been,   a dream
lining my coat pockets in its dust. i must have been foolish.
is it not worth the sacrifice of bodies that could never
enter these poems? oh   holiest hope-
filled thing, i wished   to save you
from the truth: there is no   tomorrow   here
for things like us. i say us and mean   a litany
of flies, all black, wings crusting over   the sides; i say
what if and mean   regardless   there will be
flowers but who knows for whom   they will be
grown. i speak of the trees and mean   the dead
air rapturing my hands.
and maybe it took too long   to write this.
the crows have already missed their tickets   home.

we finally get there———

after George Abraham

1.
—should we start ?
be honest, I do not know

this place
to name
it
safe. Traversing the long Atlantic
is tiring I
know

,
I know my
beloveds

will call home, I know

Finally we
count.

2.
—what part
can
we say we own What we found,

rotting devoted
beautiful trees
hydrangea-light

climbing the trunks of our
legs
we found

Nothing was ever theirs.

3.
—we will

know to steal
from a stone swallowing

endless

nowhere ; here
could be different if we
stopped believing in
all borders
if we forgot
the language of
first.

Home

when I talk about mountains
I am being romantic
about the valley
—Rio Cortez “A Class Distinction”

Impact of Return

a failed palindrome after Phillip B. Williams

Upon leaving:
By the end of the poem, I will return
to my country a new ghost, a cracked mortar

ground into the sound of freedom etching
the skin. There is so much to believe a country

is worth—its weight, the gold it harvests
from the fields, the fields it owns like the people,

its people worked like a field. When I stop
to question the way color bends around

the skin, I am only met with batons; an orchestra
of violence crescendos across my bones.

What a radical concept: freedom that drips
from the mouth of its country, a river of hymns

drifting along its banks, a small dove drinking from
this song until its feathers burst

into a shredded flag. My first country was a flame-
soaked ocean; my first country started in rot, the smell of

coins decaying the land. In the stars we found
a space, a country built of milk new as the honey

of a mother's warm blood, a land that we tend to
as it tends to us—we, the soft ground ready

to be tilled by the wind's crescent hands.
And what a beautiful sight, to call something Black

and soft and alive, children with dandelions
skittling their hair. A boy cups our moon's face

like a melon, kisses its cheeks before tumbling
back to the pillowed ground, and this is how we say

goodnight: a ritual, a dance, the skin left intact. The boy
rises from the ocean adorned in a crown of seaweed

and shells brown as his buttered eyes; I wish I could
show you the golden ring crowning his head, pelicans

swooping from the loops in his braids as the light pulls
from a single thread of hair and we all rejoice a life

here another day. And isn't that supposed to be
beautiful, too—living, a fountain of Black arms unfolding

over a stove? We let the dinner table drown in Black limbs buzzing
loud as a cicadaed August; this too becomes the work of the people,

mouths hungry for the wet sap of laughter. We chose
against a land that specialized in stealing. Today I passed

a cop car and its leather seats ribboned out a bed of flowers,
a small jungle of geraniums springing from

its dashboard. I picked one and a siren bloomed sweet
in my hand. I watch its petals bullet out towards my skin.

Upon returning:
I watch a bullet petal out towards my skin,

become a siren blooming sour in my hand, a vicious mercury

spade sifted into carob flesh. Between

the dashboard of a small car there is the dead

boy, a picked tendon, small jungle of geraniums sprung

out from a bed of flowers, his leather hide ribboning

as a cop car passes us, light spilling out like a severed vein.

This land that specializes in stealing did its job. Today

it chose against the wet sap of laughter, it worked

the people hungry, mouthed a dry

cicadaed August. This, too, becomes part of the machine:

our Black limbs buzzing loud as a glowing, white

furnace; we let the sidewalks drown in a fountain of

Black, arms folding over each other like a shield.

And isn't that supposed to be the law of living

here another day? We all mourn a life,

the light pulling from a single thread of hair,

swooping the loops in our braids as

the blonde rings crown our necks, pelicans

circling our carcasses like vultures, beaks dripping

a desire for our meat. I wish I could show you

the shells' casings, black as a dead boy's bored-in eye sockets,

an ocean adorned in our bodies, tangled with seaweed.

A ritual, a dance. The skin left haggard. A boy falls to

the pillaged ground and this is how we say *goodbye*:

kissing his cheek before he tumbles back to

the moon, his face like a melon.

A child with skittles dandelioning his hair. A boy cradles

something Black and soft and wanting to live.

Crescent hands, what a beautiful sight it was—to call

the soft ground ready to be tilled in plots.

The land that we tend to is our blood,

a country built from the milk of our mothers,

the smell of coins decaying the land in rot,

my first country soaked flames in its ocean.

My first country started as a shredded flag,

a song of a small dove bursting

into feathers. My first country was not

a country but a war. It smiled

in its own stench of blood coating its field,

dressing its people. Color can only bend

around the brightest light when that’s all there is.

I return to my first country

its bullets, its laws, the crack in its scarleting sky

and nothing more.

essay on YEET!
a road map after Simone White

if you are wondering where
        we are, here
the grass grows

        thistled and
thorned, unconcerned
        by what could cause it

harm, stupidly
        blooming everywhere it can
touch, which is everywhere

        next to the mouth
of a mothering creek, and yes
        the creeks here

bloom, too, wild
        daisy-chain of water lilying
its way around

the greening bark
of old oaks
which are still

blooming into a perfect
orange and i must mention the apples here
are so bright that even the crisp air takes

sips from them, the tangerines
bloom their sharpest
during what you once knew

as winter but we know as
nothing ever dies, we never run
out of space, the land itself cracks

a smile wide enough for us to build
on its teeth and yes here too we dance
and the dance is an act of blooming, and there

is no tomorrow or yesterday, only right now and uncles
licked in the mystique of a charcoal grill and i must have
mentioned the trees before, their vines tangled

and thriving, their trunks wet with breathing, the small
triangles of flush light peering through their leaves, it covers us
in silk as we dance, yes, this blooming

is survival, a dance
    we continue even after our music drifts

into the windbreaker whistle
    of the leaves and we dance to our own

silence, the jive-break-pop of our bodies collecting sweat
    in awe of each other's movements, all as one we dance

circles around each other, a rotating hand of a bracket clock freezing
    us in a swirled step, where we can sound out

the drop of the knees as they buckle from the soft
    age lent to us by the sand, the dust clacking

beneath our soles, our dreads a gust of tambourines boomboomcacking to the silence
    we are holding, the blade in our fingers

excavating the joy
    in the lack of noise, look how loud we have become

in all of this space, we are soaked
    in felicity, our mouths clayed

into silent laughter, we dance like Black blood
    cells suturing wounds, spiraling silence, listen, hear

the joints crack out of place, the small steps of praise
        pressing joy into the dirt, a praise so holy

ghost that we perform to this trap beat, a praise
        so grotesque that we still come out unbloodied, our snarls and yips piercing

the night, a praise of blooming bodies hollering into the dark, a praise
        only the dead could create, could you imagine

        a place loving us for being
alive, i must
        admit, this isn't a map for you

        to find us, rather to know we made it
safe, there's so much green
        in the palms of our planet that it is starting to hue

the sky, if i take a deep enough breath, my lungs will bloom wild
        orchids, their stems hugging my arteries,
it has become so difficult to say *beautiful* and not mean *alive*.

Notes

This book is a collection of imaginations. I aimed to ask the question, what does freedom look like? What does it mean to have an oppressed people gain their freedom? What happens if we all just left Earth? It sits in the lineage of Eve Ewing, Danez Smith, and Rio Cortez as a sign of Afrofuturism at its core. The title, *YEET!*, is the exploration of Blackness, and Black Language at its most fundamental, when it belonged to Black people solely. This book looks at the trajectory of language and how when it is not colonized, it remains sacred, yes, even our jokes come from a god.

"When we finally get there—" was crafted after George Abraham's VS The Podcast episode.
"This Has Never Been My america" is a Burning Haibun, a form created by torrin a. greathouse.
"Essays on "How can Black People Write About Flowers at a Time like this?" is after Hanif Abdurraqib's series of poems with the same title.
"Essay on YEET!: the invisible city" is based after Italo Calvino's poem "invisible cities" and borrows language from Waka Flocka Flame's *No Hands.*
"New World Cento" borrows language from previous poems in the book.
"Life before the war was beautiful" borrows its title from a speech given by Kuzbass Zubrii.
"Impact of Return" is a palindrome after Phillip B. Williams' "Final Poem as Tidalectic Elegy."
"*Gettin' Religion, 1948*" is an ekphrastic poem based on a painting titled the same from Archibald John Motley, Jr.

Acknowledgments

First, I would like to thank my mother for always being there and supporting me. Thank you to my little sister, Jamie. You are one of my best friends even when I told you were not. I love you both to the moon and back. Thank you to my grandpa, I always want to make you proud. To Ruth, my grandma, I love you and miss you every day, I hope these poems sing to you.

Thank you to Sawako Nakayasu for selecting my book out of countless others to be published by Omnidawn. I am continually amazed and humbled by the people who find anything when engaging with my work. Thank you to Omnidawn for this collection of hope. Rusty and Laura, I owe so much to you for believing in my poems, making a book I can be proud of, for letting my fantasy be a reality.

Thank you to my Poet Sister Taylor, I don't always believe in my work but you never let me get too down about my poems. I will always appreciate your willingness to sit with my work, crazy how we sat in my little New York apartment and edited my first book, then three years laters we did the same for this book.

Thank you to Daniel, I have one foot out the door on this and you pulled me back, thank you for reading my work with both the intensity of an editor and the kindness of a fan. Thank you Dior, for always talking through and around a poem or a problem. For you laughter when we need it most. Thank you Seamus, you work so hard to make everyone around you shine just as bright as you do, I love you, endlessly. Thank you Michelle, the OG first reader from the Ypsilanti days. Our friendship means the moon to me. Thank you to my first readers and people that touched these poems before anyone else, K., Kay, Grady, Quintin, Dia, and so many others.

Thank you to my MFA, The New School. This project was born from a dream and a workshop. Thank you to Mark Bibbins, from day one you saw what was potential and you never let me shy away from it. Thank you to Camille Rankine, J. Mae Barizo, and Elaine Equi for your classes and you words about and around my work. Thank you to the best workshop thesis group one could ever ask for, Emma, Maria, and Luopu. Y'all really sat with these poems. Forever and always to MMPR, Lannie, Ashwini, Rota, Simon, Alex, and Cozine. Shout out to the Bedstuy Baddies, TAP, Joshua, Jim, and Colby. You all bring spirit to my writing and joy to my life.

Shout out to my love that keeps me going, Stephen. I know when I need, I can reach out to you for a laugh or a cry. Words cannot express how much that means to me. Moreso, how often you check on me, even when I do not ask for it. To Anthony Cody, thank you for being so willing to guide me after the announcement of this book. I was so afraid of letting these poems go, your words comforted me.

Thank you to any place willing enough to let me read my poems, give talks, share knowledge, learn, and grow. I am the poet I am today because you allowed me space.

Dear reader, I must also thank you for engaging with this text. I hope you see the value in yourself and in Black existences. Dear you, past, present, and future, Black people exist, continue to exist, will continue to exist. If you are a person actively fighting against this known truth, know you will never win. If you are a person who needs to hear this truth, know you survive. Dear future, thank you for surviving.

Thank you to the journals and magazines that have graciously given space to other versions of these poems.

"When we finally get there—" & "History of Leaving" were published in *FogLifter* and was republished in the exquisite anthology.
"Exhaustion Theory" was published in *Cincinnati Review.*
"This has never been my america" was published in *Beestung.*
"If I ever leave New York, I am going to burn everything (I Own)" was published in *Indiana Review.*
"If I keep saying flowers in enough poems, I wonder if they will finally bloom" was published in *Exposition Review.*
"Asters" was published in *Rhino Poetry.*
"A Double Sonnet for the River" was published in *Split This Rock.*
"translations of an ancient text" was published in *The Maine Review.*
"Impact on Return" was published in *Frontier Poetry.*
"On God" was published in *Handwritten & Co.*

jason b crawford is the author of *Year of the Unicorn Kidz* from Sundress Publications. They were born in Washington DC, raised in Lansing, MI. Currently they reside in Brooklyn, NY.

YEET!
by jason b crawford

Cover photo from jason b crawford
Cover typeface: Abril Fatface

Interior design by jason b crawford and Laura Joakimson
Interior typefaces: Times New Roman and Cardo

Printed in the United States
by Books International, Dulles, Virginia
Acid Free Archival Quality Recycled Paper

Publication of this book was made possible in part by gifts from
Katherine & John Gravendyk in honor of Hillary Gravendyk,
Francesca Bell, Mary Mackey, and New Place Fund

Omnidawn Publishing Oakland, California
Staff and Volunteers, Fall 2025
Rusty Morrison & Laura Joakimson, co-publishers
Elizabeth Aeschliman, production editor
Sophia Carr, production editor
Rob Hendricks, poetry editor
Jeffrey Kingman, copy editor
Sharon Zetter, poetry editor & book designer
Anthony Cody, poetry editor
Liza Flum, poetry editor
Jennifer Metsker, marketing assistant
Avantika Chitturi, marketing assistant
Angela Liu, marketing assistant